AN ABUNDANT LIFE P...

ABUNDANT LIFE
IS *Yours!*

GET THE ABUNDANT LIFE IS YOURS! DIGITAL COURSE AVAILABLE NOW!

A PERSONAL BLUEPRINT TO HELP YOU DESIGN AND MANIFEST YOUR ABUNDANT LIFE

REBECCA LYNN POPE

COPYRIGHT DISCLAIMER

Copyright © Rebecca Lynn Pope LLC, 2022
All Rights Reserved.

Published by Rebecca Lynn Pope LLC, 4514 Chamblee Dunwoody Rd. Ste. 329, Atlanta, GA 30338

www.rebeccalynnpope.com

Formatted for publishing by Cre8 Your Reality Publishing and Simply Mena

All rights reserved. No portion of this book or any digital products contained in this book may be reproduced in any form without permission from the publisher, except as permitted by U.S. copyright law.

For permissions contact: contact@rebeccalynnpope.com

Who is REBECCA LYNN POPE?

Rebecca Lynn Pope is a spiritual powerhouse and healer who is passionate about empowering people to live abundantly. She has fought hard to overcome her own struggles and darkness so that she can help to shine light into yours. Rebecca leads and teaches what she has lived and learned from personal experience.

Rebecca is America's favorite cool and sexy aunty! She is the queen of tough love and brings a loving no-nonsense approach to life advice that is often delivered with a vicious yet hilarious side-eye.

Professionally, Rebecca is a master life and love coach, spiritual healer, pastor, bestselling author, serial entrepreneur, and influencer. She creates world-class courses on life, love, business, and leadership. Rebecca also certifies professional life coaches. She currently has over 250 certified Abundant Life Coaches around the globe. In addition, Rebecca is the host of the show Marry Me Now on the OWN network.

Rebecca Lynn lives in Atlanta, GA, and is married to her soulmate and best friend. She is the mother of three grown sons, two daughters, a granddaughter, a miniature Chihuahua, and a bad-butt little pug named Hardy.

She looks forward to personally mentoring and teaching you how to begin to get honest, get out of your own way, and start living abundantly!

Hello Love,

I am so grateful that you are joining me on this journey of self-discovery. This book is a portion of an ebook that I wrote years ago. It introduces my concept and definition of Abundant Life. You have not picked up this book by accident or coincidence. God guided you here because you have been seeking and desiring more for your life. Deep down, you know that there is more for you and that you are meant for greater. It is time to start living abundantly!

If you truly want to begin to live the life of your dreams you have to begin to let go of the fears that keep sabotaging and holding you back. Then and only then can you start manifesting your greatest desires.

I wrote this book to help you begin this work! I will be with you every step of the way sharing my own stories as inspiration.

Please keep in mind that I am known for tough love, keeping it real, and saying the things that nobody else will say. So buckle up because it is my job to challenge you.

I believe in you and I love you.

Blessings and Abundance,

Rebecca

ABUNDANT LIFE IS YOURS!

TABLE OF CONTENTS

1. BROKEN TO ABUNDANT
I went through a lot of hell before I got to my heaven. The path to peace is often paved with suffering. Don't give up and don't lose hope. It is time to heal.

2. WHAT IS ABUNDANT LIFE?
In this part, we will define Abundant Life. In order to make it the goal, we have to define what it is.

3. ABUNDANT LIFE SELF-ANALYSIS
Here, you will take a closer look at your current life so that you can determine what's working and identify the areas that need more focus and intention.

4. SUCCESS STORIES
Testimonials for Abundant Life Path courses and Rebecca Lynn Pope.

5. NOTES & REFLECTIONS
Some extra space to free-flow journal, write down reminders, and reflect on your Abundant Life homework.

GET THE DIGITAL COURSE

CLAIM YOUR SPECIAL GIFT TODAY!

~~Value $197~~

Hello Love, are you ready to get serious about manifesting your abundant life? If so, make sure to get my Abundant Life is Yours! Ecourse & Audible Affirmations to go along with this workbook. In this ecourse, I share even more of my personal stories, and manifestation tips, AND I created audible affirmations so you can listen on the go!

FOR A LIMITED TIME, GET THE ABUNDANT LIFE IS YOURS! ECOURSE FOR ONLY $47! THAT'S OVER 75% OFF! MY GIFT TO YOU FOR PURCHASING THIS WORKBOOK.

USE DISCOUNT CODE: ABUNDANCE AT CHECKOUT

GO TO WWW.REBECCALYNNPOPE.COM UNDER *COURSES* TO CLAIM YOUR SPOT TODAY!

Join This Global Healing Movement
& Help Transform Lives

Become a Certified Abundant Life Coach

CLAIM YOUR SPOT

GO TO **WWW.REBECCALYNNPOPE.COM** UNDER
BECOME A COACH TO CLAIM YOUR SPOT TODAY!

PART 1

Broken to Abundant

I went through a lot of hell before I got to my heaven. The path to peace is often paved with suffering. Don't give up and don't lose hope. It is time to heal.

MY BEAUTIFUL ABUNDANT LIFE

> ...I came that they may have life and have it abundantly.
> - John 10:10

If you ask me what Abundant Life means to me now I have a different answer than I would have ten or twenty years ago. Now, living abundantly is synonymous with joy, peace, balance, passion, purpose, and personal acceptance. It is being comfortable in my own skin and loving myself no matter what the current circumstances may look or feel like. It is spiritual alignment and a genuine relationship with God. It is having friends who are like family. It is a life of freedom; mind, body, and spirit. It is the absence of shame, guilt, or regret. It is knowing that God is with me in every moment, in every step, and that nothing can separate me from the love of God.

This place of peace and love did not manifest for me overnight. I had reached a very broken and low place in life when I began to truly seek God and answers. As a preacher's kid, I knew all about church, but I had never been taught about relationship and intimacy with God. That came through suffering and pain. It is often in suffering that we ask the right questions because we finally reach the end of our rope and are willing to listen. Listening is the key, and the only way I have learned to listen to God is through stillness. It is in the stillness that God speaks and guides.

In 2013, my mother died after a ten-year battle with ovarian cancer. She was my rock, best friend, and #1 supporter. I was lost without her. In a cloud of grief and overwhelmed with depression, I climbed into my bed and pulled the covers over my head. I stopped working, and my business went downhill. By this time, I had started my professional coaching business and had a radio show in Atlanta. My dream of building a multi-million dollar business had come true, but something was still missing. When you are young, you think that money is the answer to everything, but I learned that no matter how much money I made, I wasn't truly fulfilled or happy deep down. Something was missing.

Within a few months of my mom dying and not working, my money began to dry up, and I was living on my savings. When the eviction notice came, I threw it on top of the huge pile of bills I was ignoring and climbed back in bed. In 2014, only seven months after my mom died, I got evicted from my apartment. I was depressed, grieving, and lost. I moved in with a friend for a few weeks while I tried to get a game plan. I still had Global Rebuild, my construction supply company, I just needed to focus and handle my business which meant I needed to get over the depression, get out of bed, and get back to work.

Within a few weeks of getting evicted, Global received the largest order we had ever had. I went from dead broke to plenty of money in the blink of an eye. I got a condo and tried to get my life back together, but I was lost and confused. The eviction had thrown me. I couldn't understand how or why God had let that happen to me (victim mindset). Back in 2010, when I was on the verge of losing everything, God had made a way (by me getting off my ass and getting to work, mind you), but in my grief, I didn't see it that way. On top of my sister dying when I was 10 years old and my mom, now I felt like even God had abandoned me.

I didn't realize that all of the pain and trauma I had survived, like the death of my sister, a horrendous divorce, domestic abuse, court battles, and financial struggles, had all taken their toll. I wasn't just grieving my mother. The chickens had come home to roost. I was finally dealing with decades of unprocessed pain, anxiety, and trauma, and no amount of sex, alcohol, or burying myself in work could fix it. I had to finally face it all.

Late one night, curled up in a ball in my bed, when I was all cried out, I began to talk to God.

I prayed a prayer that I had never prayed. I said,

"God, I am lost. I don't know what I am doing or where I am going. Everything I have tried to do isn't working and has failed. I am broke, busted, and disgusted. You know me better than I know myself, and I obviously don't know what the hell I am doing. So, I give you my life. I am who you say I am. I will go where you lead me. I will say what you tell me to say. I will do what you show me to do."

From that day forward, God began to guide me into personal healing. I began to study healing techniques, read books, and finally got therapy. I learned to meditate. I made my personal well-being my top priority. I stopped trying to use alcohol and men to ease my pain. I faced it all. I began to rebuild my life, but this time from a place of peace and spiritual alignment, not desperation.

We can't heal what we deny. If you want to start living abundantly, you will have to get ruthlessly honest about what is holding you back.

My life is full of joy and purpose. I am a spiritual healer. That gets expressed in my professional life. I work for myself as a full-time spirit-led master life & love coach. I wake up every day to do what I love. I get to help people for a living! It brings me joy and deep fulfillment. To have the freedom to do what I love and live life on my terms is something I have been working towards most of my life.

Being a heart-centered entrepreneur is at the core of who I am. I create digital courses, write books, and make Youtube videos, and I even hosted a show on the Opray Winfrey network. I am the CEO of Abundant Life Path University, where we offer digital courses on life, love, business, and leadership. I have trained and certified over 250 Abundant Life Coaches worldwide.

My wealth goals have changed over the years. Money became less important as I became more aligned with true identity, peace, and the deeper meaning of my life. Of course, that is when you make more money! Lol! What you chase always has a way of evading you, but it manifests effortlessly when you allow it just to flow. Now, instead of chasing money, money chases me! Anything that I birth out of my heart makes money effortlessly or leads me to make more money. Money manifests itself through my life, passions, alignment with other enlightened souls, and desire to see those around me live abundantly.

I am in excellent health. I am not on any medications, my blood pressure is great, and my heart is healthy. I exercise regularly and eat right. I am emotionally and mentally healthy as well. I no longer suffer from anxiety and fear. My stress levels are minimal, and my self-love and confidence are at an all-time high.

In 2015, I married my soulmate and best friend, Kerry. Together, we have had to unpack and help each other heal. Relationships reveal wounds that you may not even be aware of in isolation. Healing work never ends.

I'm a boy mom. I now have three grown sons who are prospering and following their own paths. I have a brand new granddaughter Olivia Kay who is the most precious gift. I have two bonus daughters whom I love dearly and get to do all the girly stuff I feel like I missed out on raising my sons.

I have sister-friends who are like family and have helped me through some of the darkest places in my life.

I walked right into my Abundant Life, one step and one day at a time. Now, it is your turn.

Abundant Life is Yours!

THANK YOU GOD FOR ABUNDANT LIFE

THE ABUNDANT LIFE PLEDGE

SET YOUR INTENTIONS AND COMMIT TO THIS JOURNEY.

I, _____ (full name), set my intentions to begin to manifest my abundant life. I give myself permission to see myself as God sees me, through the lens of love and greatness. I commit to pushing through any and all resistance that may arise as a result of this work. I choose today to open my heart and mind to receive new ideas, new thoughts, new feelings, new ways, and new people who will align with my new abundant life. I invoke and command that all resources, provision, and opportunities are making their way toward me even now. The stars are divinely aligning right now for the grandest and most abundant version of my life to manifest.

_____   _____
Signature   Date

Your life begins to change the day you take responsibility for it.

STEVE MARABOLI

… PART 2

What is Abundant Life?

In this part, we will define Abundant Life. In order to make it the goal, we have to define what it is.

ABUNDANT LIFE

PERSONAL WELLBEING AND SUCCESS IN 5 AREAS OF LIFE: HEALTH, WEALTH, LOVE, PEACE, AND PURPOSE

5 Elements
OF ABUNDANT LIFE

- HEALTH
- WEALTH
- LOVE
- PEACE
- PURPOSE

To make Abundant Life the goal and to manifest it, we must first define it. There are five elements to Abundant Life: Health, Wealth, Love, Peace, and Purpose. These five elements are the essential components of a joyful, fulfilled, and purposeful life.

Defining Abundant Life in this way is going to help you focus on what matters to you. You will create a crystal clear vision of your dream life and then learn the mindset and habits necessary for it to manifest. Success looks different for everyone. It is up to you to get honest with yourself and dare to dream bigger than you ever have before.

Abundant Life ELEMENTS

- HEALTH
- WEALTH
- LOVE
- PEACE
- PURPOSE

YOUR AUTHENTIC & ABUNDANT DREAM LIFE

Abundant Life Defined

Health

Your physical wellbeing is crucial to living a happy and fulfilling life. For anyone currently experiencing health issues, you know that not being in good health will dominate your time, energy, and focus. It is often all you can think about. It causes stress, anxiety, and strain not just on yourself but also on those you love. It isn't easy to focus and build on the other elements of an abundant life if you aren't feeling well. If you aren't at your best physically or have gained weight and are struggling to lose it, this can affect your self-esteem and confidence. It isn't easy to separate how you feel physically from your mental and spiritual wellbeing. Your health is a crucial element to living your best life. You cannot ignore your body, health issues, or how you are feeling and expect to be happy. Your health and physical wellbeing must be a top priority in your dream life strategy.

ABUNDANT LIFE IS YOURS!

Abundant Life DEFINED

Wealth

When you say abundance to most people, their minds immediately go to money. Well, we know that financial well-being is definitely crucial to living a peaceful and enjoyable life. Financial stress can make or break relationships and marriages. Living in lack will give you sleepless nights and anxious days. It is crucial to move out of a mentality of lack and struggle in order to enjoy life. So whatever your dreams are they most definitely involve some level of financial success. Money is required to do nearly everything, but it is up to you to decide how much is needed to live the life of your dreams. In this book, you will learn that it is within your power to attract and manifest your dream money goals.

You are not mean to live in a state of struggle or continuous suffering. This serves no one. Your natural state is abundance.

> "Struggling and suffering are meant to only last for a season...not a lifetime. You must learn the lesson in order to move on." - Rebecca Lynn Pope

> **BIG-HEARTED PEOPLE OFTEN FAIL TO LOVE THEMSELVES FIRST.**

Rebecca Lynn Pope

Abundant Life Defined

Love

Love is a human need, not just a desire or want. Babies die without physical touch and affection. Humans thrive through emotional and physical connections with others. You could have all of the other elements of Abundant Life, but if you don't have love, you will feel unfulfilled. Some of you may be reading this book because you specifically want to manifest romantic love. One of my secrets to attracting love is self-love! When you focus and invest in your own wellbeing: mind, body, and spirit, it attracts others who will do the same.

So many big-hearted, compassionate, and loving people struggle to attract healthy and loving relationships because they have never learned, or been taught, to believe in themselves and their own innate self-worth. They keep trying to give away the love they should be focusing on themselves. In dating and relationships, this lack of self-worth often translates into neediness, a lack of boundaries, low self-esteem, desperation, enabling, people-pleasing, and even passive-aggressive behavior.

For those with high self-esteem, love can often be evasive because true love is connected to authenticity. Getting crystal clear and honest about who you are and what you want will clear the way for love to manifest.

Abundant Life Defined

Peace

Peace is the fundamental building block of an Abundant Life. Your peace of mind is crucial. The ability to think clearly and make sound decisions is all centered on your peace of mind. Anxiety, worry, and stress will steal your joy. You can have all the money in the world but if you can't enjoy it without worrying it means nothing. And likewise, you can be down to your last dollar but still have peace and know that you are going to be okay and everything is going to work out. Peace is the cornerstone of manifestation. Peace = Certainty = Self-Assurance = Confidence! And remember, confidence is the jet fuel for dreams!

Purpose

Purpose is what gives life deeper meaning. I encourage you to not think of purpose as one thing, an occupation, or a destination. Instead, purpose is what makes you feel fulfilled. It is not always associated with money, but it always centered around your passions. For thousands of years, humans have been searching for the meaning of life. For the sake of the exercises in this book we are going to define purpose as any activities that you love, do naturally, make you feel fulfilled, AND help people other than yourself. It is always connected to making a difference in the world. Purpose is where your passions and helping people intersect. Over time, this can evolve and change.

> **PURPOSE IS WHERE YOUR PASSIONS AND HELPING PEOPLE INTERSECT.**
>
> *Rebecca Lynn Pope*

FREE FLOW JOURNALING

WRITE DOWN/JOURNAL ALL THOUGHTS THAT YOU HAVE AS THEY SHOW UP. BE AS NON-JUDGEMENTAL AS POSSIBLE.

First Thoughts

Below, do some free flow journaling. Write down your immediate thoughts and feelings after reading my story and the definition of Abundant Life. Just write whatever comes to mind, in no particular order, and without censoring yourself.

> **YOU ARE LIMITLESS! IT IS TIME TO GET OUT OF YOUR OWN WAY.**
>
> *— Rebecca Lynn Pope*

What is Missing?

As you read the definition of Abundant Life how did it change how you think about your life and dreams? Have you been limiting yourself? Have you been focusing on one element at the expense of another? What elements have you been avoiding or neglecting?

_____
_____
_____
_____
_____
_____
_____
_____
_____
_____
_____
_____
_____
_____
_____
_____
_____

RESISTANCE

OPPOSITION OR PUSHING BACK AGAINST SUGGESTIONS, EVEN THOSE THAT COULD HELP YOU SOLVE OR IMPROVE YOUR MENTAL, SPIRITUAL, AND EMOTIONAL WELLBEING.

Get Out of Your Own Way

Did any doubts, fears, or negative self-talk come up as you begin to think about yourself and your dreams in terms of Abundance?

_____
_____
_____
_____
_____
_____
_____
_____
_____
_____
_____
_____
_____
_____
_____
_____
_____
_____

How Are You Feeling?

What are you most excited about as you begin this journey?

Abundant Life Homework

MORE FREE FLOW JOURNALING

01 BUY A NICE JOURNAL AND PEN

When I first started journaling I used random legal pads and sheets of paper, however, this is not conducive to making a habit of journaling. Using a nice pen and book will make the experience even more enjoyable and something to look forward to every day!

02 INCORPORATE JOURNALING INTO YOUR MORNING ROUTINE

Add journaling to your morning routine, like right after you pray and meditate, or right after you get a cup of coffee. (Coffee is life! I can't do anything without my first cup of coffee. Lol!)

03 KEEP YOUR JOURNAL VISIBLE

Keep your journal visible so you remember to write in it. Creating new habits requires reinforcement. When you see your journal, you will be more likely to keep picking it up. Sit it where you can see it like on your meditation pillow or on the nightstand next to your bed.

04 JOURNAL IN THE SAME SPOT EVERY DAY

Journaling in the same spot will make it easier to make journaling a long-term habit which is the goal. it a habit and stick to it long term, which in the end is the goal of starting a journal in the first place.

05 DON'T OVERTHINK

Your journal is private. It is for yourself. Not anyone else. When you write, don't filter or censor yourself. You don't have to be afraid, or ashamed. It is a judgment-free zone! Let your thoughts run onto paper so that you can revisit them for yourself whenever you feel like it.

Scientifically Proven

BENEFITS OF JOURNALING

01 REDUCE STRESS

Writing out your feelings about stressful events is proven to reduce stress.

02 REDUCE DEPRESSION

Journaling can be as effective as cognitive behavioral therapy to reduce depression and anxiety.

03 BOOST YOUR IMMUNE SYSTEM

People who journal for at least 20 minutes a day, 3-5 times per week, get less sick.

04 INCREASES GRATITUDE

People who journal have a more holistic perspective about their lives which cultivates gratitude.

05 TRAUMA RECOVERY

Writing things down helps you to focus on the good even when there is bad. It also helps you to face pain instead of denying it.

06 IMPROVE MEMORY

"The practice of writing can enhance the brain's intake, processing, retaining, and retrieving of information." - Judy Willis

> NEVER GIVE UP ON WHAT YOU REALLY WANT TO DO. THE PERSON WITH BIG DREAMS IS MORE POWERFUL THAN ONE WITH ALL THE FACTS.

Albert Einstein

PART 3

Abundant Life Self-Anaylis

In this part, you will take a closer look at your current life so that you can determine what's working and identify the areas that need more focus and intention.

Abundant Life CIRCLE

This exercise is designed to take a snapshot of your current life across specific categories, including the five elements of Abundant Life. I have used this tool for years to help coaching clients determine what is working versus what areas need more work. The first time I used this tool myself I was shocked to realize that I was unhappy/unfulfilled in a couple areas where I thought I was doing okay. The key is to be honest with yourself. We can't heal what we deny. Give a rating from 1 to 10 in each category below, one being you're "totally unsatisfied" and ten being you're "completely satisfied and killing it"!

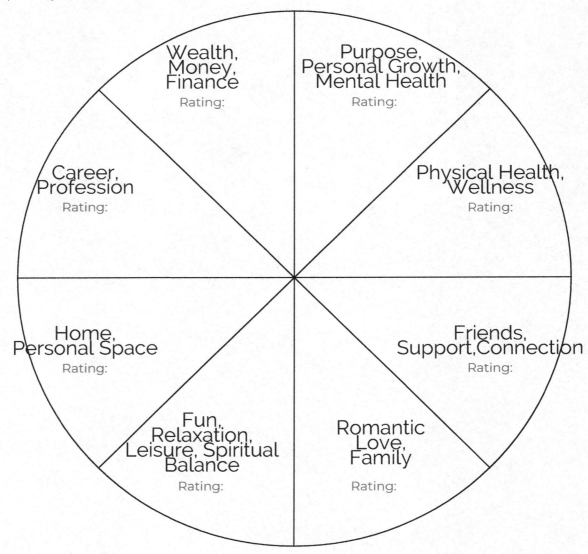

WHAT IS WORKING 1
Abundant Life Analysis

In this section, circle your rating for each category on a scale of 1 to 10. In each category, write down what you're happy with and what is working. Even if you aren't where you want to be in an area, think about what you have changed or what you are doing better. It is important to identify the mindsets, habits, and behaviors that we are working well for you even if you aren't at your ultimate goal.

Career/Profession	Wealth/Money/Finance
01 02 03 04 05 06 07 08 09 10	01 02 03 04 05 06 07 08 09 10
What are you happy with & what is working?	What are you happy with & what is working?

Purpose/Personal Growth/ Mental Health	Physical Health/Wellness
01 02 03 04 05 06 07 08 09 10	01 02 03 04 05 06 07 08 09 10
What are you happy with & what is working?	What are you happy with & what is working?

WHAT IS WORKING 2

Abundant Life Analysis

In this section, circle your rating for each category on a scale of 1 to 10. In each category, write down what you're happy with and what is working. Even if you aren't where you want to be in an area, think about what you have changed or what you are doing better. It is important to identify the mindsets, habits, and behaviors that we are working well for you even if you aren't at your ultimate goal.

Friends/Support/Connection

01	02	03	04	05	06	07	08	09	10

What are you happy with & what is working?

Romantic Love/Family

01	02	03	04	05	06	07	08	09	10

What are you happy with & what is working?

Fun/Relaxation/Leisure/Spiritual Balance

01	02	03	04	05	06	07	08	09	10

What are you happy with & what is working?

Home/Personal Space

01	02	03	04	05	06	07	08	09	10

What are you happy with & what is working?

HOW CAN YOU IMPROVE?
Abundant Life Analysis

In each category, identify tasks or actions you can take right away to start seeing improvement.

Career/Profession	Wealth/Money/Finance
Purpose/Personal Growth/Mental Health	Physical Health/Wellness
Friends/Support/Connection	Romantic Love/Family
Fun/Relaxation/Leisure/Spiritual Balance	Home/Personal Space

> **ACKNOWLEDING THE GOOD THAT YOU ALREADY HAVE IN YOUR LIFE IS THE FOUNDATION FOR ALL ABUNDANCE.**
>
> — *Eckhart Tolle*

Abundant Life Self-Analysis Tip

WORK ON THE CATEGORIES WHERE YOU ARE MOST SUCCESSFUL FIRST AND THEN MOVE ON TO THE CATEGORIES WHERE YOU SCORED LOWEST.

#ABUNDANTLIFE

Abundant Life CAREER

Career & Profession

Q&A WORKSHEET 1

CURRENT SCORE: _____

Let's drill down to get more insight. Answer the following questions about this category of your life to help identify what needs to change.

DID YOUR SCORE IN THIS AREA SURPRISE YOU? IF SO, WHY?

HAVE YOU BEEN IGNORING THIS AREA OF YOUR LIFE? IF SO, WHY?

HOW DO YOU FEEL WHEN YOU THINK ABOUT WHAT IT IS GOING TO TAKE TO SEE IMPROVEMENT IN THIS AREA? EXCITED? ANXIOUS? WORRIED? WHY?

Career & Profession
Q&A WORKSHEET 2

WHAT IS YOUR CURRENT LEVEL OF SELF-CONFIDENCE IN THIS AREA? DO YOU FEEL EMPOWERED, DISCOURAGED, OVERWHELMED? WHY?

HOW DO YOU TALK TO YOURSELF IN THIS AREA? IS YOUR SELF-TALK POSITIVE, UPLIFTING, ENCOURAGING? OR NEGATIVE, DEFEATED, DISCOURAGING?

Career & Profession
Q&A WORKSHEET 3

WHAT CAN YOU DO TO IMPROVE YOUR MINDSET AND SELF-CONFIDENCE IN THIS AREA?

WHAT ACTION(S) CAN YOU TAKE IMMEDIATELY TO INCREASE YOUR SCORE IN THIS AREA BY 1 POINT?

Career & Profession
POSITIVE AFFIRMATIONS

- I AM CAPABLE!
- I LOVE WHAT I DO FOR A LIVING!
- I ACHIEVE MY GOALS!
- I AM AN ASSET!
- DOORS ARE OPENING!
- I CAN DO THIS!

Practice the Affirmations

Take 3 deep cleansing breaths, exhaling slowly with each breath. Now say each of the Wealth, Money, & Finance Positive Affirmations out loud. Repeat each one slowly three times each. Focus on how each one makes you feel. In the space below, write down your response to each affirmation. Which one makes you feel empowered or maybe even a little scared? **This is your ABUNDANT CAREER AFFIRMATION.** Write it below. You will use this one affirmation consistently to help improve your mindset and confidence about your dream profession. Practice by saying it out loud an additional 20 times!

CAREER AFFIRMATION

In the space below, practice writing out your Abundant Career Affirmation. The more times you speak and write the affirmation the more effective it will be in reprogramming your brain for Abundance.

> "DOING WHAT YOU LOVE IS THE CORNERSTONE OF HAVING ABUNDANCE IN YOUR LIFE."
>
> — *Wayne Dyer*

Manifestation Tip

USE THE THOUGHT SHIFTING TECHNIQUE ALONG WITH YOUR POSITIVE AFFIRMATION TO COUNTERACT NEGATIVE SELF-TALK AND HEAL YOUR MINDSET.

#ABUNDANTLIFE

Career & Profession
DREAM VISION 1

What does the career or profession of your dreams look like? What are you doing? How much money do you make?

Career & Profession
DREAM VISION 2

Describe what a day in your dream career or profession looks like. What time do you wake up? How many hours do you work? What do you wear? Where do you work? What kind of people do you work with? Describe it in vivid detail as if what you write is going to manifest!

Career & Profession
DREAM VISION BOARD

Let's visualize it! Create a vision board of what your dream career looks like. Is there someone you can identify who is currently doing your dream career/profession? If so, attach a picture of them below along with other pictures, words, quotes, etc., that represent your dream.

Career & Profession
PLANNER
ABUNDANT LIFE SELF-ANALYSIS

SHORT-TERM GOAL:

LONG-TERM GOAL:

OBSTACLES THAT NEED TO BE OVERCOME:

IMMEDIATE TASKS FOR SHORT-TERM GOAL:

_____

_____

_____

_____

_____

_____

BOOKS, TOOLS, RESOURCES, RESEARCH, & SUPPORT NEEDED FOR LONG TERM IMPROVEMENT:

Career & Profession

CURRENT SCORE: _____   **DREAM SCORE: _____**

Use this space to DREAM A LITTLE MORE! Make notes, brainstorm, do some free flow journaling, or write out your Abundant Career Affirmation as many times as you want to start reprogramming your brain for Abundance!

Abundant Life
WEALTH, MONEY, FINANCE

Wealth, Money, & Finance

Q&A WORKSHEET 1
CURRENT SCORE: _____

Let's drill down to get more insight. Answer the following questions about this category of your life to help identify what needs to change.

DID YOUR SCORE IN THIS AREA SURPRISE YOU? IF SO, WHY?

HAVE YOU BEEN IGNORING THIS AREA OF YOUR LIFE? IF SO, WHY?

HOW DO YOU FEEL WHEN YOU THINK ABOUT WHAT IT IS GOING TO TAKE TO SEE IMPROVEMENT IN THIS AREA? EXCITED? ANXIOUS? WORRIED? WHY?

Wealth, Money, & Finance

Q&A WORKSHEET 2

WHAT IS YOUR CURRENT LEVEL OF SELF-CONFIDENCE IN THIS AREA? DO YOU FEEL EMPOWERED, DISCOURAGED, OVERWHELMED? WHY?

HOW DO YOU TALK TO YOURSELF IN THIS AREA? IS YOUR SELF-TALK POSITIVE, UPLIFTING, ENCOURAGING? OR NEGATIVE, DEFEATED, DISCOURAGING?

Wealth, Money, & Finance
Q&A WORKSHEET 3

WHAT CAN YOU DO TO IMPROVE YOUR MINDSET AND SELF-CONFIDENCE IN THIS AREA?

WHAT ACTION(S) CAN YOU TAKE IMMEDIATELY TO INCREASE YOUR SCORE IN THIS AREA BY 1 POINT?

> "YOU DESERVE TO HAVE A PROSPEROUS AND ABUNDANT LIFE."
>
> *Lynn Robinson*

Wealth, Money, & Finance
POSITIVE AFFIRMATIONS

- I AM WEALTHY!
- I COMMIT TO MY MONEY DREAMS!
- I HAVE MORE THAN ENOUGH!
- WEALTH IS COMING TO ME IN UNEXPECTED WAYS!
- I DESERVE A LIFE OF FINANCIAL ABUNDANCE!
- MULTIPLE STREAMS OF INCOME IS MY NEW NORMAL!

Practice the Affirmations

Take 3 deep cleansing breaths, exhaling slowly with each breath. Now say each of the Wealth, Money, & Finance Positive Affirmations out loud. Repeat each one slowly three times each. Focus on how each one makes you feel. In the space below, write down your response to each affirmation. Which one makes you feel empowered or maybe even a little scared? **This is your ABUNDANT MONEY AFFIRMATION.** Write it below. You will use this one affirmation consistently to help improve your mindset and confidence. Practice by saying it out loud an additional 20 times!

Your Abundant
MONEY AFFIRMATION

In the space below, practice writing out your Abundant Money Affirmation. The more times you speak and write the affirmation the more effective it will be in reprogramming your brain for Abundance.

Manifestation Tip

IT IS THE REPETITION OF POSITIVE AFFIRMATIONS THAT REPROGRAMS YOUR BRAIN FOR ABUNDANCE.

#ABUNDANTLIFE

Wealth, Money, & Finance
DREAM VISION 1

What does the wealth and money of your dreams look like? How much money do you make? Credit score? How much money is in savings? How much are you worth? What do you own?

Wealth, Money, & Finance
DREAM VISION 2

Describe what a day in your life looks like when you have the wealth and money of your dreams? Where will you go? What will you do? Where will you live? What will you do with an abundance of money? Describe it in vivid detail as if what you write is going to manifest!

Wealth, Money, & Finance
DREAM VISION BOARD

Let's visualize it! Create a vision board of what your dream wealth and money looks like. Use pictures, words, quotes, etc., that represent your dream.

Wealth, Money, & Finance
PLANNER

ABUNDANT LIFE SELF-ANALYSIS

SHORT-TERM GOAL:

IMMEDIATE TASKS FOR SHORT-TERM GOAL:

_____

_____

_____

_____

_____

LONG-TERM GOAL:

OBSTACLES THAT NEED TO BE OVERCOME:

BOOKS, TOOLS, RESOURCES, RESEARCH, & SUPPORT NEEDED FOR LONG TERM IMPROVEMENT:

Wealth, Money, & Finance

CURRENT SCORE: _____   DREAM SCORE: _____

Use this space to DREAM A LITTLE MORE! Make notes, brainstorm, do some free flow journaling, or write out your Abundant Money Affirmation as many times as you want to start reprogramming your brain for Abundance!

Abundant Life
PURPOSE, PERSONAL GROWTH, AND MENTAL HEALTH

Purpose & Personal Growth

Q&A WORKSHEET 1

CURRENT SCORE: _____

Let's drill down to get more insight. Answer the following questions about this category of your life to help identify what needs to change.

DID YOUR SCORE IN THIS AREA SURPRISE YOU? IF SO, WHY?

HAVE YOU BEEN IGNORING THIS AREA OF YOUR LIFE? IF SO, WHY?

HOW DO YOU FEEL WHEN YOU THINK ABOUT WHAT IT IS GOING TO TAKE TO SEE IMPROVEMENT IN THIS AREA? EXCITED? ANXIOUS? WORRIED? WHY?

Purpose & Personal Growth

Q&A WORKSHEET 2

WHAT IS YOUR CURRENT LEVEL OF SELF-CONFIDENCE IN THIS AREA? DO YOU FEEL EMPOWERED, DISCOURAGED, OVERWHELMED? WHY?

HOW DO YOU TALK TO YOURSELF IN THIS AREA? IS YOUR SELF-TALK POSITIVE, UPLIFTING, ENCOURAGING? OR NEGATIVE, DEFEATED, DISCOURAGING?

Purpose & Personal Growth

Q&A WORKSHEET 3

WHAT CAN YOU DO TO IMPROVE YOUR MINDSET AND SELF-CONFIDENCE IN THIS AREA?

WHAT ACTION(S) CAN YOU TAKE IMMEDIATELY TO INCREASE YOUR SCORE IN THIS AREA BY 1 POINT?

Purpose & Personal Growth
POSITIVE AFFIRMATIONS

- AS I FOLLOW MY HEART I WALK IN PURPOSE
- I COMMIT TO BEING THE BEST ME THAT I CAN BE
- I DO THE HARD THINGS
- I ASK FOR HELP WHEN I NEED IT
- SELF-AWARENESS IS THE KEY THAT UNLOCKS HEALING
- EVERY DAY AND IN EVERY WAY I AM GETTING BETTER AND BETTER

Practice the Affirmations

Take 3 deep cleansing breaths, exhaling slowly with each breath. Now say each of the Purpose & Personal Growth Positive Affirmations out loud. Repeat each one slowly three times each. Focus on how each one makes you feel. In the space below, write down your response to each affirmation. Which one makes you feel empowered or maybe even a little scared? **This is your ABUNDANT PERSONAL GROWTH AFFIRMATION.** Write it below. You will use this one affirmation consistently to help improve your mindset and confidence. Practice by saying it out loud an additional 20 times!

PERSONAL GROWTH AFFIRMATION

In the space below, practice writing out your Abundant Personal Growth Affirmation. The more times you speak and write the affirmation the more effective it will be in reprogramming your brain for Abundance.

Manifestation Tip

SO WITHIN, SO WITHOUT...HOW YOU THINK AND FEEL ABOUT YOURSELF IS CREATING YOUR LIFE.

#ABUNDANTLIFE

Purpose & Personal Growth
DREAM VISION 1

What does purpose, personal growth, and the mental health of your dreams look like? What will believing in yourself and making yourself a top priority manifest in your life? How will people treat you? How will you show up? What will you accomplish? What new things will you try? How will you dare to dream bigger?

Purpose & Personal Growth
DREAM VISION 2

Describe what a day in your life looks like when you are healed to the next level and loving yourself? What does self-care and self-love look like for you? Do you go to therapy regularly? Do you read self-help books? Take life coaching courses? What will happen if you stop doubting yourself, putting yourself down, or self-sabotaging? Describe it in vivid detail as if what you write is going to manifest!

Purpose & Personal Growth

DREAM VISION BOARD

Let's visualize it! Create a vision board of what your dream YOU looks like. Use pictures, words, quotes, etc., that represent you living your best life with healthy boundaries, self-esteem, and self-confidence.

> "AN ABUNDANT LIFE IS ONE WHERE WE ARE PHYSICALLY STRONG, MENTALLY SOUND, AND SPIRITUALLY AFLAME."
>
> — *Toni Sorenson*

Purpose & Personal Growth
PLANNER
ABUNDANT LIFE SELF-ANALYSIS

SHORT-TERM GOAL:

LONG-TERM GOAL:

OBSTACLES THAT NEED TO BE OVERCOME:

IMMEDIATE TASKS FOR SHORT-TERM GOAL:
_____
_____
_____
_____
_____
_____
_____

BOOKS, TOOLS, RESOURCES, RESEARCH, & SUPPORT NEEDED FOR LONG TERM IMPROVEMENT:

Purpose & Personal Growth

CURRENT SCORE: _____   DREAM SCORE: _____

Use this space to DREAM A LITTLE MORE! Make notes, brainstorm, do some free flow journaling, or write out your Abundant Personal Growth Affirmation as many times as you want to start reprogramming your brain for Abundance!

Abundant Life
PHYSICAL HEALTH & WELLNESS

Physical Health & Wellness

Q&A WORKSHEET 1
CURRENT SCORE: _____

Let's drill down to get more insight. Answer the following questions about this category of your life to help identify what needs to change.

DID YOUR SCORE IN THIS AREA SURPRISE YOU? IF SO, WHY?

HAVE YOU BEEN IGNORING THIS AREA OF YOUR LIFE? IF SO, WHY?

HOW DO YOU FEEL WHEN YOU THINK ABOUT WHAT IT IS GOING TO TAKE TO SEE IMPROVEMENT IN THIS AREA? EXCITED? ANXIOUS? WORRIED? WHY?

Physical Health & Wellness

Q&A WORKSHEET 2

WHAT IS YOUR CURRENT LEVEL OF SELF-CONFIDENCE IN THIS AREA? DO YOU FEEL EMPOWERED, DISCOURAGED, OVERWHELMED? WHY?

HOW DO YOU TALK TO YOURSELF IN THIS AREA? IS YOUR SELF-TALK POSITIVE, UPLIFTING, ENCOURAGING? OR NEGATIVE, DEFEATED, DISCOURAGING?

Physical Health & Wellness

Q&A WORKSHEET 3

WHAT CAN YOU DO TO IMPROVE YOUR MINDSET AND SELF-CONFIDENCE IN THIS AREA?

WHAT ACTION(S) CAN YOU TAKE IMMEDIATELY TO INCREASE YOUR SCORE IN THIS AREA BY 1 POINT?

Physical Health & Wellness

POSITIVE AFFIRMATIONS

- MY BODY IS HEALTHY, STRONG & THRIVING!
- TAKING CARE OF MY BODY IS SELF-CARE!
- I AM FULL OF ENERGY!
- I HONOR MY BODY WITH HEALTHY DIET & EXERCISE!
- I SAY YES TO HEALTH AND PERSONAL WELLBEING!
- I MAKE MY HEALTH A TOP PRIORITY EVERY DAY!

Practice the Affirmations

Take 3 deep cleansing breaths, exhaling slowly with each breath. Now say each of the Physical Health & Wellness Positive Affirmations out loud. Repeat each one slowly three times each. Focus on how each one makes you feel. In the space below, write down your response to each affirmation. Which one makes you feel empowered or maybe even a little scared? **This is your ABUNDANT PHYSICAL HEALTH & WELLNESS AFFIRMATION.** Write it below. You will use this one affirmation consistently to help improve your mindset and confidence. Practice by saying it out loud an additional 20 times!

Your Abundant
PHYSICAL HEALTH AFFIRMATION

In the space below, practice writing out your Abundant Physical Health & Wellness Affirmation. The more times you speak and write the affirmation the more effective it will be in reprogramming your brain for Abundance.

> **HEALTH IS WEALTH.**

Unknown

Manifestation Tip

TAKING CARE OF YOURSELF PHYSICALLY SIGNALS THE UNIVERSE THAT YOU ARE MAKING YOUR WELLBEING A TOP PRIORITY AND WILL RESPOND WITH MORE WELLNESS & WHOLENESS IN THE OTHER AREAS.

#ABUNDANTLIFE

Physical Health & Wellness

DREAM VISION 1

What does the physical health and wellness of your dreams look like? What will a strong and healthy body change in your life? How will you feel about yourself? What will you do? How will you dress? How will it change how you show up? Will you try something new?

Physical Health & Wellness

DREAM VISION 2

Describe what a day in your life looks like when you are physically strong, healthy, and loving your body. How will you take care of your body? What do you do for exercise? What do you eat? How do you feel? Describe it in vivid detail as if what you write is going to manifest!

Physical Health & Wellness
DREAM VISION BOARD

Let's visualize it! Create a vision board of what the physical health & wellness of your dreams looks like. Use pictures, words, quotes, etc., that represent you looking and feeling great physically.

Physical Health & Wellness
PLANNER
ABUNDANT LIFE SELF-ANALYSIS

SHORT-TERM GOAL:

LONG-TERM GOAL:

OBSTACLES THAT NEED TO BE OVERCOME:

IMMEDIATE TASKS FOR SHORT-TERM GOAL:

_____

_____

_____

_____

_____

_____

BOOKS, TOOLS, RESOURCES, RESEARCH, & SUPPORT NEEDED FOR LONG TERM IMPROVEMENT:

Physical Health & Wellness

CURRENT SCORE: _____   DREAM SCORE: _____

Use this space to DREAM A LITTLE MORE! Make notes, brainstorm, do some free flow journaling, or write out your Abundant Physical Health & Wellness Affirmation as many times as you want to start reprogramming your brain for Abundance!

Abundant Life
FRIENDS, SUPPORT, & CONNECTION

Friends, Support, & Connection
Q&A WORKSHEET 1

CURRENT SCORE: _____

Let's drill down to get more insight. Answer the following questions about this category of your life to help identify what needs to change.

DID YOUR SCORE IN THIS AREA SURPRISE YOU? IF SO, WHY?

HAVE YOU BEEN IGNORING THIS AREA OF YOUR LIFE? IF SO, WHY?

HOW DO YOU FEEL WHEN YOU THINK ABOUT WHAT IT IS GOING TO TAKE TO SEE IMPROVEMENT IN THIS AREA? EXCITED? ANXIOUS? WORRIED? WHY?

Friends, Support, & Connection
Q&A WORKSHEET 2

WHAT IS YOUR CURRENT LEVEL OF SELF-CONFIDENCE IN THIS AREA? DO YOU FEEL EMPOWERED, DISCOURAGED, OVERWHELMED? WHY?

HOW DO YOU TALK TO YOURSELF IN THIS AREA? IS YOUR SELF-TALK POSITIVE, UPLIFTING, ENCOURAGING? OR NEGATIVE, DEFEATED, DISCOURAGING?

Friends, Support, & Connection
Q&A WORKSHEET 3

WHAT CAN YOU DO TO IMPROVE YOUR MINDSET AND SELF-CONFIDENCE IN THIS AREA?

WHAT ACTION(S) CAN YOU TAKE IMMEDIATELY TO INCREASE YOUR SCORE IN THIS AREA BY 1 POINT?

Friends, Support, & Connection
POSITIVE AFFIRMATIONS

- I AM A GREAT FRIEND!
- I HAVE LOVING FRIENDSHIPS THAT I VALUE!
- I AM LOVED AND SUPPORTED!
- I LET GO OF TOXIC PEOPLE IN MY LIFE!
- I SAY YES TO HEALTHY AND LOVING FRIENDSHIPS!
- I AM HONEST, OPEN, AND AUTHENTIC WITH MY FRIENDS!

Practice the Affirmations

Take 3 deep cleansing breaths, exhaling slowly with each breath. Now say each of the Physical Health & Wellness Positive Affirmations out loud. Repeat each one slowly three times each. Focus on how each one makes you feel. In the space below, write down your response to each affirmation. Which one makes you feel empowered or maybe even a little scared? **This is your ABUNDANT FRIENDS & SUPPORT AFFIRMATION.** Write it below. You will use this one affirmation consistently to help improve your mindset and confidence. Practice by saying it out loud an additional 20 times!

FRIENDS & SUPPORT AFFIRMATION

In the space below, practice writing out your Abundant Friends & Support Affirmation. The more times you speak and write the affirmation the more effective it will be in reprogramming your brain for Abundance.

_____
_____
_____
_____
_____
_____
_____
_____
_____
_____
_____
_____
_____
_____
_____
_____
_____
_____

Manifestation Tip

YOU ARE AN AVERAGE OF THE FIVE PEOPLE CLOSEST TO YOU. CHOOSE YOUR FRIENDS AND ENERGY WISELY. THE COMPANY WE KEEP MATTERS GREATLY WHEN IT COMES TO MANIFESTING.

#ABUNDANTLIFE

Friends, Support, & Connection
DREAM VISION 1

What do the friends, support, and connections of your dreams look like? How will you feel in these friendships? How will you be treated? What activities will you and your friends do together? What will you talk about? What will you share? How will being open, honest, authentic, and trusting in friendships help you live your dream life?

Friends, Support, & Connection

DREAM VISION 2

Describe what a day in your life looks like when you are loved and have great friendships? Describe it in vivid detail as if what you write is going to manifest!

ABUNDANT LIFE IS YOURS!

Friends, Support, & Connection

DREAM VISION BOARD

Let's visualize it! Create a vision board of what the friendships, support, and connections of your dreams looks and feels like. Use pictures, words, quotes, etc., that represent your life with these healthy and loving relationships.

Friends, Support, & Connection
PLANNER
ABUNDANT LIFE SELF-ANALYSIS

SHORT-TERM GOAL:

IMMEDIATE TASKS FOR SHORT-TERM GOAL:

_____

_____

LONG-TERM GOAL:

_____

_____

_____

OBSTACLES THAT NEED TO BE OVERCOME:

BOOKS, TOOLS, RESOURCES, RESEARCH, & SUPPORT NEEDED FOR LONG TERM IMPROVEMENT:

Friends, Support, & Connection

CURRENT SCORE: _____   DREAM SCORE: _____

Use this space to DREAM A LITTLE MORE! Make notes, brainstorm, do some free flow journaling, or write out your Abundant Friends & Support Affirmation as many times as you want to start reprogramming your brain for Abundance!

Abundant Life
ROMANTIC LOVE & FAMILY

Romantic Love & Family
Q&A WORKSHEET 1
CURRENT SCORE: _____

Let's drill down to get more insight. Answer the following questions about this category of your life to help identify what needs to change.

DID YOUR SCORE IN THIS AREA SURPRISE YOU? IF SO, WHY?

HAVE YOU BEEN IGNORING THIS AREA OF YOUR LIFE? IF SO, WHY?

HOW DO YOU FEEL WHEN YOU THINK ABOUT WHAT IT IS GOING TO TAKE TO SEE IMPROVEMENT IN THIS AREA? EXCITED? ANXIOUS? WORRIED? WHY?

Romantic Love & Family
Q&A WORKSHEET 2

WHAT IS YOUR CURRENT LEVEL OF SELF-CONFIDENCE IN THIS AREA? DO YOU FEEL EMPOWERED, DISCOURAGED, OVERWHELMED? WHY?

HOW DO YOU TALK TO YOURSELF IN THIS AREA? IS YOUR SELF-TALK POSITIVE, UPLIFTING, ENCOURAGING? OR NEGATIVE, DEFEATED, DISCOURAGING?

Romantic Love & Family

Q&A WORKSHEET 3

WHAT CAN YOU DO TO IMPROVE YOUR MINDSET AND SELF-CONFIDENCE IN THIS AREA?

WHAT ACTION(S) CAN YOU TAKE IMMEDIATELY TO INCREASE YOUR SCORE IN THIS AREA BY 1 POINT?

> **ALIGN WITH LOVE AND TAP INTO ABUNDANCE.**
>
> *Unknown*

Romantic Love & Family
POSITIVE AFFIRMATIONS

I AM LOVABLE!	**I DESERVE TO GIVE & RECEIVE HEALTHY LOVE!**
MY HEART IS PREPARED TO RECEIVE LOVE!	**I ONLY ATTRACT HEALTHY AND LOVING RELATION-SHIPS!**
HEALTHY RELATION-SHIPS DO NOT REQUIRE ME TO LOSE MYSELF	**I CHOOSE TO MINIMIZE RELATION-SHIPS THAT ARE TOXIC OR UNENJOYABLE**

Practice the Affirmations

Take 3 deep cleansing breaths, exhaling slowly with each breath. Now say each of the Physical Health & Wellness Positive Affirmations out loud. Repeat each one slowly three times each. Focus on how each one makes you feel. In the space below, write down your response to each affirmation. Which one makes you feel empowered or maybe even a little scared? **This is your ABUNDANT LOVE & FAMILY AFFIRMATION.** Write it below. You will use this one affirmation consistently to help improve your mindset and confidence. Practice by saying it out loud an additional 20 times!

Your Abundant
LOVE & FAMILY AFFIRMATION

In the space below, practice writing out your Abundant Love & Family Affirmation. The more times you speak and write the affirmation the more effective it will be in reprogramming your brain for Abundance.

Manifestation Tip

THE QUALITY OF OUR RELATIONSHIPS IS DIRECTLY CONNECTED TO OUR PERSONAL LEVEL OF SELF-ESTEEM, HEALING, & SELF-CONFIDENCE. WORK ON YOURSELF IN ORDER TO MANIFEST HEALTHIER RELATIONSHIPS.

#ABUNDANTLIFE

Romantic Love & Family

DREAM VISION 1

Please note: we don't get to choose what families we are born into and it is not your responsibility to heal your family if they are not wanting to clean up their side of the street. We cannot make our family members become loving and healthy. If they aren't willing participants God can give you new people who will be like the family of your dreams.

How will you feel when you have the romantic love and family relationships of your dreams? How will you be treated? What activities will you and your loved ones do together? What will you talk about? What will you and your romantic partner do together? Describe your dream life.

Romantic Love & Family
DREAM VISION 2

Describe what a day in your life looks like when you are in love and have close family relationships? Describe it in vivid detail as if what you write is going to manifest!

Romantic Love & Family
DREAM VISION BOARD

Let's visualize it! Create a vision board of what romantic love and the family of your dreams looks and feels like. Use pictures, words, quotes, etc., that represent your life with these healthy and loving relationships.

Romantic Love & Family Planner

ABUNDANT LIFE SELF-ANALYSIS

SHORT-TERM GOAL:

LONG-TERM GOAL:

OBSTACLES THAT NEED TO BE OVERCOME:

IMMEDIATE TASKS FOR SHORT-TERM GOAL:

_____

_____

_____

_____

_____

_____

_____

BOOKS, TOOLS, RESOURCES, RESEARCH, & SUPPORT NEEDED FOR LONG TERM IMPROVEMENT:

ABUNDANT LIFE IS YOURS!

Romantic Love & Family

CURRENT SCORE: _____   DREAM SCORE: _____

Use this space to DREAM A LITTLE MORE! Make notes, brainstorm, do some free flow journaling, or write out your Abundant Love & Family Affirmation as many times as you want to start reprogramming your brain for Abundance!

Abundant Life
FUN, RELAXATION, LEISURE, HOBBIES, & SPIRITUAL BALANCE

Fun, Relaxation, & Hobbies

Q&A WORKSHEET 1

CURRENT SCORE: _____

Let's drill down to get more insight. Answer the following questions about this category of your life to help identify what needs to change.

DID YOUR SCORE IN THIS AREA SURPRISE YOU? IF SO, WHY?

HAVE YOU BEEN IGNORING THIS AREA OF YOUR LIFE? IF SO, WHY?

HOW DO YOU FEEL WHEN YOU THINK ABOUT WHAT IT IS GOING TO TAKE TO SEE IMPROVEMENT IN THIS AREA? EXCITED? ANXIOUS? WORRIED? WHY?

Fun, Relaxation, & Hobbies

Q&A WORKSHEET 2

WHAT IS YOUR CURRENT LEVEL OF SELF-CONFIDENCE IN THIS AREA? DO YOU FEEL EMPOWERED, DISCOURAGED, OVERWHELMED? WHY?

HOW DO YOU TALK TO YOURSELF IN THIS AREA? IS YOUR SELF-TALK POSITIVE, UPLIFTING, ENCOURAGING? OR NEGATIVE, DEFEATED, DISCOURAGING?

Fun, Relaxation, & Hobbies
Q&A WORKSHEET 3

WHAT CAN YOU DO TO IMPROVE YOUR MINDSET AND SELF-CONFIDENCE IN THIS AREA?

WHAT ACTION(S) CAN YOU TAKE IMMEDIATELY TO INCREASE YOUR SCORE IN THIS AREA BY 1 POINT?

Fun, Relaxation, & Hobbies
POSITIVE AFFIRMATIONS

- REST AND FUN ARE A CRUCIAL PART OF AN ABUNDANT LIFE
- I AM CREATING A LIFE FULL OF FUN, LAUGHTER, AND JOY
- I WILL FOLLOW MY BLISS
- IT IS WHEN I RELAX THAT I CONNECT WITH GOD
- I WORK HARD SO I CAN PLAY HARDER
- I GIVE MYSELF PERMISSION TO TRY NEW THINGS

Practice the Affirmations

Take 3 deep cleansing breaths, exhaling slowly with each breath. Now say each of the Physical Health & Wellness Positive Affirmations out loud. Repeat each one slowly three times each. Focus on how each one makes you feel. In the space below, write down your response to each affirmation. Which one makes you feel empowered or maybe even a little scared? **This is your ABUNDANT FUN & RELAXATION AFFIRMATION.** Write it below. You will use this one affirmation consistently to help improve your mindset and confidence. Practice by saying it out loud an additional 20 times!

FUN & RELAXATION AFFIRMATION

In the space below, practice writing out your Abundant Fun & Relaxation Affirmation. The more times you speak and write the affirmation the more effective it will be in reprogramming your brain for Abundance.

Manifestation Tip

LIFE IS MEANT TO BE WELL-LIVED. YOU ARE MEANT TO DO MORE THAN PAY BILLS AND DIE. I CHALLENGE YOU TO START MAKING FUN AN ACTUAL LIFE GOAL. JOY ATTRACTS ABUNDANCE!

#ABUNDANTLIFE

Fun, Relaxation, & Hobbies

DREAM VISION 1

What does the most fun and relaxed version of your dream life look like? Can you see yourself smiling and laughing? What hobbies do you love? What new hobbies would you like to try? Who are you laughing with? Are you ready to follow your bliss? How will it feel to embrace joy and remove stress, worry, and anxiety? Describe your dream life in terms of fun, relaxation, leisure, hobbies, and spiritual balance.

Fun, Relaxation, & Hobbies

DREAM VISION 2

Describe what a day in your life looks like when you are less worried and stressed. What does work-life balance look like in your dreams? If you are a workaholic (like me) what will your dream life feel when you actually take time to enjoy the fruits of your labor? Another side effect of relaxing is that you get to live in the moment and enjoy your life and loved ones. How will that feel? Describe it in vivid detail as if what you write is going to manifest!

Fun, Relaxation, & Hobbies

DREAM VISION BOARD

Let's visualize it! Create a vision board of what fun, relaxation, and the bliss of your dreams looks and feels like. Use pictures, words, quotes, etc., that represent your fun and well-balanced life.

> LIFE IS MEANT TO BE ABUNDANT IN ALL AREAS.
>
> — Rhonda Byrne

Fun, Relaxation, & Hobbies
PLANNER
ABUNDANT LIFE SELF-ANALYSIS

SHORT-TERM GOAL:

IMMEDIATE TASKS FOR SHORT-TERM GOAL:

LONG-TERM GOAL:

_____

_____

_____

_____

_____

OBSTACLES THAT NEED TO BE OVERCOME:

BOOKS, TOOLS, RESOURCES, RESEARCH, & SUPPORT NEEDED FOR LONG TERM IMPROVEMENT:

Fun, Relaxation, & Hobbies

CURRENT SCORE: _____   DREAM SCORE: _____

Use this space to DREAM A LITTLE MORE! Make notes, brainstorm, do some free flow journaling, or write out your Abundant Fun & Relaxation Affirmation as many times as you want to start reprogramming your brain for Abundance!

PART 4

Success Stories

Testimonials from clients and coaches for Abundant Life Path courses and Rebecca Lynn Pope.

Abundant Life Path
TESTIMONIALS

I had the pleasure of meeting Mrs. Rebecca and Mr. Pope via Facebook about 5 years ago. I had no idea how my life would change after deciding to become a student of the dynamic duo!

Let me start by saying my actual soul was suffering because of the hurt and pain I had endured here on this journey of life. I was stressed, depressed, lost, broke, and broken. I was being tormented by the bad selections and experiences of my past. I was overweight and had 3 and 4 jobs just to make ends meet; that was not life and living. I was existing and very burnt out.

I can never forget how I had reached a breaking point in my life, and Mrs. Rebecca told me she would help me to heal. I had no idea if this would work or not. However, I was desperate for happiness, peace, joy, and relief in my life. Now, this was about 5 years ago, keep in mind.

Since then, my life has done a complete turnaround for the better.
Like night and day!

The courses, workshops, workbooks, retreats, certifications, etc., are well worth it. The material and teachings have helped me grow in many ways. I'm beyond grateful for God giving her this vision to help others and train others on how to help others.
The more healing released In the world, the merrier it will be for all parties involved.

I recommend ALPU, and its phenomenal leader Rebecca Lynn Pope to everybody who feels called to lead, coach, preach and teach. These two are so loving and selfless. They walk and live in the spirit of excellence.

- Jymesha Yapelle

Abundant Life Path
TESTIMONIALS

Connecting with Rebecca has been life-changing! She has not only given me the tools to change my life but also provided me with continued support and love throughout my journey. When I first met Rebecca, I was recently divorced and full of pain. I was juggling my full-time job and trying to be a good mom, but the daily grind and pain were just too heavy. I was tired of doing the same thing with no results! Rebecca guided me through my healing and gave me the courage to find myself! Today my life is FLIPPED! I am a Certified Abundant Life Coach and full-time business owner. I was able to quit my 9 to 5 and create the life I want and love! I will forever be grateful to Rebecca for helping me flip my life!
- Andrea L. Cooks

Working with Rebecca helped change my life forever. I was broken and at a lost place after the breakup of my husband and me of 18.5 years in 2019. This certification @ ALPU in 2020 not only help healed my broken heart but held me accountable for doing my inner healing work and owning my truth. It also helped me with the confidence in building my low self-esteem I have today to finding my lane, picking back up the pieces of my life, & finding my purpose path back to God; as now a certified Abundant Life Coach, Women's Empowerment Coach, Best Selling Author, & my continuing journey of becoming a Transformational Speaker! I give God credit and glory for bringing Rebecca Lynn to my life.

- Toshia Lane

Abundant Life Path
TESTIMONIALS

I can't thank Rebecca enough. I have so much love, respect, and appreciation for her work. I first discovered Rebecca on a YouTube video about Dating as a Boss Woman.

I quickly started following everything she created. Since then, I have completed her Healing Course, "The Work Master Class." I would give it a 5-star rating. Rebecca teaches life-changing tools that, if integrated, can heal your soul.

I have also graduated from their Certified Abundant Life Coaching Course. Wow! What an experience! I was a bit nervous at first because it was a large investment. I quickly discovered that it was everything I needed to become a confident Online Life Coach.

Her Abundant Life Coach Certification not only teaches the business side of things. It also calls each participant to grow personally and spiritually. I have gained confidence, knowledge, healing, business and marketing tools, friendships, and networking with a like-minded community.

I was so pleased with their courses, guidance, and results that I signed up for their Abundant Master Life Coaching Course. I signed up and paid before I knew all the details. Please note that I don't make irrational decisions regarding time or money.

Rebecca GIVES AND DELIVER so much Value!!!! I trust her. I am honored to be part of an honest, loving spirit-led movement. I look forward to learning more and working with her to serve, guide, and heal our online and in-person coaching clients. As part of the Abundant Life Coaching Community, I offer Life and Financial Coaching with an emphasis on credit repair, debt payoff, home buying preparation, and lifestyle design through intentional planning.

- Megan Lynn

Abundant Life Path
TESTIMONIALS

As many others have shared, working with Rebecca has been life-changing! The life I'm living now is one I couldn't even see for myself several years ago. I attended a healing circle and met my husband shortly after that. It was the beginning of me trusting myself and practicing vulnerability. I feel empowered to do the work I've been called to do. Thank you for leading and lighting the path of possibilities!

PS. I'll share pics from our May 1st wedding date when we receive them! Thank you for the many ways you enriched my life!

- Jessica Humphries

You're never to old to learn!!!! I saw a post on Facebook in 2015. I was 47. I felt useless because of my past and my life at that time. Rebecca gave me a better understanding of life's journey and healing. I now know the true responsibility of emotionally taking care of my heart and not being concerned with pleasing people. I've also learned how to vet, date and travel without guilt.

Happily married since 2018 and living the way I should have. Thankful & grateful! Love you, RLP thank you for your contribution to love, life, and people.

- Selena Johnson

Abundant Life Path
TESTIMONIALS

Rebecca has a way of looking directly into your soul and helping you pull out the best version of yourself. Expect growth, change & a ton of personal development. She's honest, open, and real. She shares her entire life with the world in hopes of helping others see a way through their trauma and life experiences. So often, the world wants to shut out the spiritual aspects of life. Abundant Life Nation coaches & courses involve a holistic approach to building the whole person's mind, body & soul. She builds you up so that you can go out and help others. It's a beautiful process. You learn so much. They are a wealth of knowledge.
- Nicole Duncan

My life has changed IMMENSELY since working with Rebecca Lynn Pope! I had some very challenging experiences that I was working through when I found her via one of her YouTube videos in 2017. I immediately booked a consultation and have been with her ever since! I worked through a divorce and a toxic relationship and learned so much about myself in the process...including the importance of self-care, self-love, and self-worth. I valued my experience so much that I became a Certified Abundant Life Coach myself! With everything I have learned from Rebecca and Abundant Life Path University, I am now the version of me that I always wanted to be and can help others become the best version of themselves and live their best life - out loud!!
- Dr. Shermnae Jones

Abundant Life Path

TESTIMONIALS

I have been beyond BLESSED by Rebecca, Kerry, and ALPU, and I am so thankful. I attended Healing 101 in 2014 and met Rebecca for the first time, and that life-changing experience became the beautiful start of my healing journey. Over the years, I've needed Life Coaching and Guidance from both Kerry and Rebecca, and their sessions were always transformative for me. These sessions would cause me to work out past traumas, hold myself and others around me accountable, and rediscover The Confident Spiritual Warrior I am.

In 2020, I took the leap of faith to become a Certified Abundant Life Coach and went through ALPCC. Becoming an Abundant Life Coach allowed me to pull back many more layers and become more aligned with my most authentic self and my REAL purpose!

What I admire the most about Rebecca & Kerry is that they are REAL, and they don't just "talk the talk" they've done their own healing work as well and will move mountains to help guide you through your journey.

It's honestly the transparency for me! ALN is a safe space filled with other like-minded individuals who want better and want to help the world become a better place. I can go on and on about these two and ALN, but if you are feeling an urge in your spirit to be a part of this movement, LISTEN to it and answer the call! It will be one of the BEST decisions you've ever made! Release ALL fear and BE PREPARED to live a life full of Abundance!

- Brittnee Wilder

PART 5

Notes & Reflections

Some extra space to free flow journal, write down reminders, reflect on your Abundant Life homework.

Notes & Reflections

Notes & Reflections

Notes & Reflections

Notes & Reflections

Notes & Reflections

Notes & Reflections

Notes & Reflections

Notes & Reflections

Notes & Reflections

Notes & Reflections

Formatted for publishing by

Publishing and More...

Contact Simply Mena
Cre8yourrealiT@gmail.com
770-276-9100

Made in the USA
Coppell, TX
31 October 2022